CAKE

T.J HUNT

 FriesenPress

One Printers Way
Altona, MB R0G 0B0
Canada

www.friesenpress.com

ISBN
978-1-03-914915-1 (Hardcover)
978-1-03-914914-4 (Paperback)
978-1-03-914916-8 (eBook)

1. BIOGRAPHY & AUTOBIOGRAPHY, PERSONAL MEMOIRS

Distributed to the trade by The Ingram Book Company

David Mckee

I hope you enjoy these slices of local love as you continue supporting with Passion your CAKE !

Thank you for being a part of the Launch

"You Matter"

Sept 19-22

Prologue

You know, God has a big job, looking out for people on earth and in heaven. I mean, I can only just imagine. We have this responsibility to make sure our lives are taking each step, making his responsibilities a little easier, making this heaven on earth.

Do I believe in God? Belief is one thing—to have faith in something that you can't see or touch, but is it the sacred feeling of God's presence?

Yes, I believe, and when times are weak or plentiful, I pray that next morning there is enough cream and sugar for the morning's coffee fuel. And seeing there's just enough—Amen!

While we're on this subject of life, there are lots of life's lessons, and I hold the pen, or in this case my mini iPad with a Bluetooth keyboard, to write my story. Each of us has a journey. The map of our life, school, marriage, work goals. We lose sight of the real passions of life.

Nobody changes standing still. Sometimes we must do what makes us uncomfortable, evolve. We need to put work into it, take chances, believe we can, because we can. It's never too late to make self-reflection a priority.

"You have two hands, one to help yourself, and one to help others."

—Audrey Hepburn

CAKE – Community And Kindness and all of the Extras!

I want to share my story, *CAKE*, with you and tell you how it has evolved with so many ingredients. I found *CAKE* fit the mold as a title. Community love and kindness matter, with positive impacts, and all of life's extras. I hope you'll enjoy all the ingredients of me.

My life experiences allowed me to look deep, grow deeper, learn, keep being tested to limits through life's lessons, over and over again, repeatedly.

When you see a fork in the road, grab it, and have some CAKE.

This book is dedicated to the memory of my mom, Diane.

I can still hear, at times, her infectious laugh and her tears; she is proud of my words. She is love.
It is also for my mom's saviour, my dad.
My children, you are love. You are the most valuable pieces of me.
To all those who have been a part of my CAKE.
It is also for those who have lost themselves and are fighting their way back.
I love you.

Chapter 1
Birthday CAKE

I love birthdays, especially mine.

I couldn't wait, as this was my day, celebrating me, feeling the love, feeling like I mattered, being surprised by delicious cake, and being around those I loved. I am Aquarius. We are forward-thinking people who want to make the world a better place. Every year, my birthday was the only day that I didn't feel like I had to reward anyone for their time to be with me, but I still did try. I insisted Mom give me treat bags with my party invitations. She said, "No, they will get treat bags at your party." I took her double mint gum from our everything drawer and handed each person a stick of gum with their invitation.

This chapter is the lead-in, like a new Netflix series—some first episodes are longer, like this chapter. But it's ok, guys. It's so that we have a good start, and you can see how it all evolves!

Every day was a new page for me; I felt I was writing my days, and I wanted to get in as much as I could. Between me and you, I thought I was living in a TV series. As I grew, I really did not know how TV worked. I started closing the bathroom door just in case a family was tuning in. I know. My mind. Instead of asking how TV worked, my brain made its own assumptions. If you have met me this makes sense—it fits who I am. Perhaps you have in your mind a visual sense of me from my introduction, even without the physical meet-up.

I was the dynamite, sometimes explosive, as I didn't know how to steady my high energy—my mind dominant and defiant. One evening I remember I asked Mom what was for dinner, and she replied, "Bacon and Eggs." My response was, "Oh my god, we're poor; poor people have breakfast for dinner." Then without hesitation, I grabbed a KitKat chocolate bar from our candy drawer, planted myself on the floor of our living room, and watched an episode of *Yan Can Cook* on the TV. I was in my leave-me-alone state; that meant no breakfast for dinner. If something set me off, I'd regret it hours later and calm myself down, processing that this was not good response. I would apologize, and in time, it became one of my routines. My shyness and good nature would shine to others, and Mom used to say, "Why are you so nice to everyone else?" I'd reply, "They can't ground me."

I found my style at a young age. I was not the girl who wanted to wear pretty dresses; instead, I found comfort in my knickers, which are what you would call capris, but with elastic bottoms, paired with my favourite brown velvet sweater, with an added accessory of a Picard Peanuts button, and pink high-top shoes. I didn't want my hair long with ribbon and bows; I felt comfortable in a short cut. My smile is what I still wear today, always in style.

I felt, at times, like an adult in a child's body. I would "play smoke" with my Nan's cigarettes. She would have cigarettes in glass cups all around her condo. Sometimes, I would light them up. It felt so natural. She was the Nan who fuelled and controlled her environment, and all those around her. My sister and I became her girlfriends, more than granddaughters. We would have lunch dates and shopping dates, and she would give us cigarette wallets, which looked like long change purses with a pocket in front for a lighter. This all seemed so natural to me, my comfort zone. I was just five years old. At the end of her life, she left her only child, my mom, nothing. Gave it all to her oxygen delivery boy and her hairdresser. My Nan controlled her own life until she passed away. It was all about her, and so it was for her to control her last breath, alone with herself. She refused to see my mom on her last days. She valued herself more than the blessings of life, even the life she created, my mom.

It is with the blessings of my life, I thank the Lord I didn't follow in her footsteps.

My other Nan allowed us to be us. She fostered our questions and our curiosity. She taught me that family was most important, and the joy in breaking bread was in the value of the company. "You should always be pulling up more chairs to your dining room table," she used to say. I took that to heart as I became an adult. Our table was always overflowing at our family gatherings, and I still carry on that tradition. She taught me to cook and clean, and whenever I tried to save room for dessert, she said, "Dessert's the same as your dinner, so finish up what you have." Nan sure could throw in sarcastic laughs.

She also covered my tracks when our family rented a cottage, just a weekend away with the family. That day she was responsible for me; we chose to hang out and cook. I thought it was a good idea to move the furniture, playing interior designer. I just couldn't sit still. I cracked the window with the couch and air was coming through it. My grandma threw her oven mitts down, moved the couch with me to align it with the crack and put on tape to seal it. It still cracks me up—she was a great accomplice. She was in her 90s when she died, still too young. Humour was her longevity, and with a grateful heart, she felt the full blessings of her whole family surrounding her.

It is with the blessings of my life, I thank the Lord I did follow in her footsteps.

Our family of four would sometimes expand with pets. Sometimes dogs, sometimes guinea pigs, hamsters, even a pigeon. I never really got attached to pets. I was a kid—at certain times of the day, I loved them, then I got bored very easily, moving on to something else.

Our house was in the middle of the street, a small street with lots of neighbourhood kids, but none of us had best friends in the group. Back then, you had neighbour friends, school friends, and best friends. We did not attend the same schools, and we were not all the same ages. We were like the"Little Rascals," or "Rug Rats," and we went home when the streetlights came on. No one was there to text us (no mobile devices); we were let out to play from daylight to dusk. Bath, then snacks—our routine. Bedtime snacks consisted of peanuts in one Dixie cup and pop in another. I remember my sister and I would make the pop last longer by sticking our finger in it and sucking the liquid off our fingers instead of drinking it. Sometimes we just drank it straight up, then lights out.

Bedtime for me was rough. I'd beg my sister to let me crawl into her bed, which by the way was literally three feet away. When she wouldn't let me, I'd scream fire, just to make her give in and let me crawl in. Yes, I also had less dramatic options. I'd sometimes sneak out of bed and curl up on a step and fall asleep, until my parents came to bed and carried me to mine (I was asleep by then and more likely to stay in my bed). Plan B: I'd wait until they went to bed and crawl into their bed. One night while doing this, I had gum in my mouth, and when we all woke up, my dad was covered in gum. I was in bubble double trouble. When sleepovers started, it was like heaven—I was never alone. But we barely slept, so we called it a "stay over."

The street was our wild playground. Hide and seek kept us busy for hours. My dad, who was working at Sears, would bring us the latest yard toys, jungle gyms, and swing sets. He even built us stilts. One time, with his crafty hands, he created a homemade long jump bar with a mattress to land on, and we flew from our feet over the bars. Monkey bar climbers and swing sets, again in the streets and yards, our wild places. Wild imaginations; what a childhood. Kids would move away, and new ones would come into the group, welcomed by me—no shocker there! I had no trouble with introductions. I was a little neighborhood watch, the street's youngest mayor!

My curiosity would lead my five-year-old self between two fold-out loungers that I tipped sideways to create a little space; a private space that fit me and one of the neighborhood boys nicely. This was where, with anticipation, I would say those nine magic words, "I'll show you mine if you show me yours!" What happened next? Me sitting in my room until supper was called—that was after I saw his pirate, I mean privates.

The next childhood moment I remember was a driveway moment. The driveway was shared with our neighbours. I guess this was another side of my personality, and not the sweet side. I was not afraid of confrontation, and for one of the many moments I recall, my mom heard screams and crying. I entered the house with a lock of hair in my fists from the neighbour's daughter's head, out of breath and dirty tears running down my face. I showed myself to my room that day. I remember it was because she drew on my new white pants with driveway chalk. I have no idea why; I just remember the act.

I seem to have such fond memories and fond moments. One of those was playing "private investigator." We played this in our garage, but we needed supplies, and the perfect time to get them was back-to-school time. We would do thumbprints by drawing on our thumbs with pen, and then putting it on paper to document the "who done it." That was a neighborhood fan favourite which, by the way, followed bible camp. In the winter months, my dad would build cupboards and a mini kitchen for our playhouse, and a door that was attached to the wall that ran along the stairs. This was our beginner playhouse (we used it until the new bigger playhouse, our stand-alone play kitchen, was built). We even drew a number on the door and drew a TV in the playhouse. We thought we were so good at interior design, even back then.

When new neighbours moved in, I played it cool. I got on my bike and went back and forth as the movers went inside the newly sold home with boxes. I tried to figure out which grown-ups might be the parents and looked to see if I could see any kids. This took patience and skill, to stay on my bike slow and steady. Then I would stop and smile hoping the lady coming out was the mom. Jackpot—it was!

I introduced myself, and she said, "Would you like to meet our girls?" My heart grew, and I could not help but grin and smile. I threw my bike down and said, "Lead the way!" To this day, I remain in contact with the girls, even after their parents passed. My heart is full, such fond memories. We got a lot of "togethers": chicken pox, straight As (okay, I didn't, but we celebrated all the same), opened our advent calendars together, and played Abba records in view of their dad who was watching golf in the other room.

Together, we filled our oversized purses with goodies to take into the movie theatre. The one time we made a day of it, we spent all day—matinees turned into the late shows. The door was open, and we were kids; it was thrilling times in the 80s.

My best friends were the ones that helped me in my roles of dating, makeup, womanhood, and getting me drunk (insert googly-eye and wine emojis). One time (no, not at band camp), I made Kool-Aid punch at a party and my friends spiked it. Let's just say that I didn't care much for alcohol; I had no idea they had spiked it. The next day, I felt like I had broken through a brick wall just like the Kool-Aid Man, but I felt like I went headfirst, breaking the wall. My head hurt, and I succumbed to my bed. My dad picked me up from that party, and I would not shut up (more than normal). That's what alcohol did to me. Next thing I know, my dad is calling me the "Kool-Aid kid." To this day, my dad still insists on calling me that.

There was one other time I tried alcohol. A girl from another school brought a small Tupperware dish with a lid—the dish's proper use was for salad dressing. I took a sip, spit it out, and said, "Why are you giving me rubbing alcohol?" She responded, "It's vodka." It was gross and burned—why on earth would people drink this? Later I learned that it wasn't so much the taste as it was the effects. I do not want to lose myself, or most important, get another nickname.

Growing up, I applied myself hard in school, but for my sister, it came more naturally. We were never compared in grades; my parents fostered our individual growth. We were two separate people. I was more high-needs. Was that fair? No, but I can't justify how I learned or my abilities—I was just me. This was how I was born. I was an average student, more hands-on and visual, which makes sense for an entrepreneur. What I envisioned was to be married forever, have children, and be a teacher. I got so much more. I experienced life. I was blessed through many experiences, with lives that are an extension of me. I'm super proud of all my children, and I'm proud of me. That's hard sometimes to say. I lost myself in moments of uncertainty but fought my way back.

I learned passion is energy.

If we never start, we never move. If we don't try, we never know.

Don't stand still—live your life with passion.

I love to love, and I love to be loved. I match energy. I'm still that girl who gets my fuel from this. Break-ups left my heart broken, and so to prevent heartbreak, I stopped dating, and sold chips and pop at the dances so I wouldn't ever feel rejected. If I could say something to my teenage self, I'd say, "Keep being you and keep selling those chips because you know your worth, even at that young age."

I lost that worth as I became an adult.

Chapter 2
Eleven Candles

Age eleven is when I started to come into my own—to become my real self. I knew I wanted to be a part of great things; I couldn't wait to be a grown up like my sister.

I couldn't wait to get a job; I was so envious of my sister, who was just shy of being three years older than me. If you have been the youngest, you know it sucks so bad—seeing the firsts through the eyes of a preteen when your sibling reaches all the fun ages before you do. So jealous of her—being the first for everything set her up for success every time. Was I the worst little sister? Perhaps, if anyone's asking, I may have been, but not with bad intentions.

I always wanted what she had, maybe because she was such a cool big sister, but I showed her in all the wrong ways. I'd sneak to her room and borrow her clothes (she was in high school I was still a junior at middle school), and then put her clothes back in her drawer before she got home. This did not stop at clothes. I also did this with jewelry and hair curling irons and make up—okay, perhaps just lip gloss. I was not that sneaky. One day my friend snapped a pic of me, and it was sitting on my dresser for anyone to see. My sister glanced down at the picture and saw me wearing her top. Busted, as they say, and she was angry. Age eleven was the year I was banned from my sister's room.

Little sisters are the gifts not too many ask for but get anyway. Like getting a knitted sweater from Aunt Bethany: cute, itchy, didn't want it, but it was a gift, and you must hang onto it forever. But as you grow up, the sweater grows on you. Like sisterly love!

We became closer as we became parents, and through our marriages. We became best friends; as they grew, we grew, and our kids were so close in age. It was so cool to have close relationships within the family! Our kids were more like extended brothers and sisters than cousins. We helped ground the roots for them by having stability and strong heathy relationships around them.

We became even closer when my mom got diagnosed with cancer.

Cancer is, well, an extension of the devil, demon to the body, an uncalled force. My mother wasn't a drinker, nor a smoker. Cancer doesn't discriminate—it dominates. When I was younger, seniors died from cancer if they smoked or drank. Now it's so widespread to all ages.

Genetic testing was suggested, as my mom's relatives all passed away from a form of cancer. So, my sister asked if we could be tested. My sister tested positive with the BRAC1 mutation, and I was negative. The day we got our call with our results, my mom had just passed away, on that very day.

CAKE

Everyone wants to write a book; it's taking the time to do so. My sister wrote one, perhaps for therapy, and to help those on the same journey. My sister went through the same surgeries as Angelina Jolie, but many years later. I wonder to this day if Angelina bought herself a copy of my sister's book. My sister got a full mastectomy, both breasts taken out, and she opted for implants. I never really knew the strength of my sister, and I never met a hero until I saw her survival of the process she underwent. She saved her own life. She is a gift to herself. My mom was our teacher of strength and passion.

Everyone should write their story. People live so many different lives, but some of us can relate and learn and take from those experiences—that is why there are writers and readers, and wisdom to learn and gain. I have enjoyed a couple of books recently—my last read was *Tuesdays with Morrie* by Mitch Albom. I suggest if you haven't soared into the pages of this, that you do! What a spark of insight to life. A perspective for all things good, challenges to do better, be better.

Chapter 3
Eighteen Candles

My first marriage, like many, was supposed to be The One, but my reality was not yet revealed. It would end as Not the Only.

Cue the karaoke and the pool balls. Yes, that should give you an introduction into our introduction.

I met my first love in a bar.

I was blonde, eighteen years old, skinny, with tiny proportions. I felt my body was underdeveloped. I had a shy personality with a spark, and a social energy that came out when I felt in my comfort zone. I was the bartender, the youngest contender there, and not much exposed to the atmosphere. When people my age were partying or sneaking into bars in high school, I was working the bar, while putting in as many hours at the Golden Arches.

Working at McDonald's was a huge playground for social teamwork building, and I grew and excelled in that family friendly environment. Passion to please! I don't mean to toot my own golden horn, but I was awarded, within months of working, crew person of the month three times and crew person of the year. I thought I'd be a lifer, but maps change.

Back to the bar...

In walk the regulars like clockwork, right as the door opens. Regulars would be waiting in their cars, just making it to the sound of the lock turning and the open sign lighting up.

I met him about a week after I started, and it was my first experience of a flirt. He would stand at the bar till closing, and sometimes join in to play pool.

He was slender in build, like me, and he had long dark hair that grew to the middle of his back.

On karaoke night, I turned the lights down low. My shift ended just before karaoke began, and my friends came to join me. Sharing our out-of-tune-voices, our audience of maybe ten people would join us in this simple pleasure.

My future husband was at the bar; he came in shortly after the music started. He took a space at the bar and ordered his drink, a Labatt's Blue.

While I was on stage, he watched me with a smile as I sang "Grandpa" by The Judds. I had a raspy voice, and somehow I was asked on many occasions if I had lived in Brooklyn.

When I read books, I just love to let my imagination flow into the description of people and what they look like. I was petite, blonde, and had a raspy voice—some people used to say I looked like Kristen Dunst, and like her role in Spider-Man, my love life was just starting a web in my heart.

After my friends left, I stayed to talk to the other bartender ladies. My future husband pulled his stool up beside me and we just started talking lightly. After some time passed, he walked me to my car and kissed me. That sealed the deal. A guy took the time to flirt with me, walk me to my car, and kiss me!

He was the first to introduce me to coffee. I have always loved the smell but hated the taste, until I started making a solution that was a balance of sweet and bold. Nowadays, it's what you would call a "triple-triple."

He lived at home. He was five years older than me, married before, no kids, and had been single for a year. I was caught in a bubble of love and life choices.

I always wanted a family of my own. I got that very young, but fast-tracking life is not the way from within your heart...

...love and energy are.

Before I continue writing I must get some sleep. Who knew typing into an iPad would make my eyes really sleepy? As they used to say in TV programs, To be continued." (Back then, there was no Netflix to binge through episodes.) We all had to painfully wait till next week. Even though I'm making you wait, it will continue as if I had not; if you're reading this, by now the book's done! But like all other writers, I have my own style—to keep you a part of the whole journey as I write, sleep, and drink coffee.

Within a year we would drive to Florida, with this being my first relationship. I was smart; I did everything I thought was right. My parents knew where I was every second and they instilled morals, so with this fresh new young love, I did go to my doctor to seek birth control. Smart. But when we came back from Florida, I brought back more than souvenirs—I brought a baby in my belly. Right. How? But at that time, like Madonna sang these words in her song, "Papa don't Preach," I never thought twice. "I'm keeping my baby."

I dreaded the talk with my mom. I remember sitting out on the patio, asking her to join me. She came out, and next thing I know, I'm in tears and she's questioning me on what my plans are. She said, "It's not only you who's pregnant, you both are." My dad had only met him once; now here's his baby with a baby and a partner he's barely met. My mom headed for the driveway, and grabbing her purse, she left. I thought about her feelings as a mother getting this news. I thought I had hurt her, and that broke my heart.

It turned out it wasn't my news that had caused her to leave. I found out she had left to go to a doctor's appointment—it's the next part that broke me. Late that evening, she said those three words, "I have cancer." Her results came back the same day I told her the news of my pregnancy. She looked at my firstborn as an angel and blessing of life that would be a strength in her fight.

My husband and I married three years later in 1996, the year I finished college. His choices—beyond my control—distracted our lives. We separated eleven months later. I found a small apartment and within a week, I left with a van, my son, clothes enough for both of us, and whatever toys I could fit in a garbage bag. Later, I went back for a couple pieces of furniture and toys, but I didn't have the fight for what I was worth, so I left him the house and the majority of items. My mentally strength meant more. I had to continue working multiple jobs: cleaning, serving at Tim Hortons three days a week, and teaching part-time at a local school. I had to keep going because the alternative was to break. I didn't break free from him completely because of my young naive mind and empathic heart.

Even after I left, I tried to make it work. I gave it my all, the last bit of fuel I had, but I soon realized this was not healthy for me in mind, body, and soul. I was two months pregnant with our second when I broke it off for good, my heart and spirit truly broken. We were just on two different roads. I thought he was on the same road—our road. But that fork seemed to have planted itself right between us, with cement.

It's been twenty-eight years since then, and I still remember the smells of that bar where we met, the busy sounds of the people, the scratches of the mic, the bands, and the regulars. To this day, some are still regulars, even though bar has changed hands quite a few times, and some have passed away. It's like going back to that scene in *Titanic*. You can still see them at the stools, and some regulars still like clockwork frequent the bar. I have only been back to that bar a handful of times, but each time I go, I am reminded that, at one time, this was my life.

In the bittersweet of things, God willingly gave me strength to allow my ex-husband to continue a relationship with our children, and heal, not just me, but both of us.

Trust in whatever process heals you—a band-aid went on that day. He was the father of my children, so I forgave him. He gave me gifts of life.

I didn't know it then, but I would go on to create something that would last forever.

A positive impact.

Chapter 4
Angel CAKE

Cancer, what a horrific word. Even seeing it, saying it, is horrific. It's like an instant bad taste in your mouth. My mom was such a gift. She had an infectious smile and laugh. She grew up in an unkind family, a controlling mother and an alcoholic father. We were just eleven and fourteen when my mom shared her true childhood. A cup of tea, peanut butter on toast, and *The Young and the Restless*.

That was the tie that binds—the most time we spent together. Just the girls—my mom, my sister, and me. The moment we all invested all our attention on Victor and Nikki and the Newman empire. None of us spoke, yet we could feel the fuel and power of the show. We loved every minute but the commercials. That was our pause to pee.

Even as we grew into adults, this connected us still. We would call each other from our own homes to share the latest who-did-what and said-what and all the drama and can-you-believe-he-did-that and she-did-that and how it was the maid's daughter's cousin's boyfriend's sister that kidnapped the baby from Nikki.

I just take a breath and try hard not to think about her death and always remember her light.

My mom was just 53.

Oprah was a light to my mom and shared her days with her. She helped bring inspiration into her life.

I was just six years young when I experienced the loss of a grandparent. My heart broke for me, but for more for my mom. That is when I think my empath heart and mind were developing. I was taking on the human feelings of others—her loss was my loss. I thought, "This was her dad, and he is no longer here for her. What sadness for her. Will she be ok?" I needed to know in my little heart that she would be ok.

I crawled my tiny self up to my mom and wrapped my arms around her as she sat in her velvet La-Z-Boy rocker and curled up on her lap, hoping she could feel my heart and know that I felt her pain. Hugs do say a lot. A hug with our hearts touching, as we sit tightly in each other's arms. A heart hug.

The casket lay open, his body still.

I will never get this image out of my head. I don't think we ever do.

I must be honest. The thought of death overwhelms me. Upon my arrival in heaven, is there a gate? Are all those who passed away before me there? Well, not everyone who passed away before me, because I don't know all of them. I'm talking about family and friends. What if no one got the memo that I'm coming, and no one is there because they're off on their wings? You see the struggle I'm having—remember, I have never been alone. Ever. Or now here's a possibility…

… do I go into the bright light they speak of (you've all heard about the bright light) without my sunglasses and end up coming through another birth canal. Another life to live, another mission.

My mom's first diagnosis with breast cancer was in her early forties and cancer came back again when she was forty-nine. She did the treatments; she did them with the strength to fight, to live her best life. One thing cancer couldn't take was her passion for life.

My parents met on a blind date. They married when my mom was eighteen years old and my dad was seventeen years old. Back in those days, he needed written permission from my grandparents to marry. They married young, and then came my sister in a baby carriage. Love, marriage, carriage, thirty-six years of marriage, two kids, five grandchildren, and fifty-three when she passed away. Her life complete. She had been a part of all our lives. They were an extension of hers.

In her last year, I took a leave of absence from my job to help support her with social visits and her daily needs. My dad had to continue working to pay for her medications—some were very costly—but he never missed an appointment. He was by her side; we all were for every chemo treatment and drain treatment. Her body wasn't just fighting one cancer, the breast cancer from five years prior, but when it came back (she learned about it in an appointment, thinking she had pneumonia), cancer fluid was draining into her lungs, and ovarian cancer showed up a year later. Because of the risks of any surgery causing her lungs to give out, they had to drain all the fluids as well as giving her chemo. Cancer's an asshole.

There were many lunch dates with my mom. I remember on one of our dates at the Golden Griddle, which became one of her favourite places to go after her treatments. Her last year and last months revolved around her preparation. Not that she knew. In fact, she told the oncologist that she didn't want to know her prognosis. She didn't want the cancer to have full control of her knowing. She didn't want cancer to win. In fact, in one of our talks, I asked why she chose cremation, and she simply said, "In the end, I want to burn cancer." She went on to say, "Cells grow in a dead body," and she didn't want the cancer to still control her after she died. She was a realistic soul in her decision, and I honoured that. She did request that we not have a funeral, but we needed that, so we honoured us. She's a forgiving woman also.

Cancer can trick easily; cancer can be manipulative. She had her moments of aging and then she'd grow hair back and glow. She had situations where she had close calls and then bounced back. She had moments of appetite and moments of food tasting like metal. Countless appointments, shots, drains—she truly was living to fight for every single day. I went through the motions. I suffered depression; as an empath, it couldn't escape me. I became part of each moment—like watching as they performed a procedure to remove the fluids, one of the effects of ovarian cancer. This caused swelling that made her balloon as if she was nine months pregnant. They suctioned litres of fluid, which drained into glass bottles, through tubes in the side of her stomach. My mom always smiled; she was so calm, her bravery, her sighs of instant relief, all during the fight to endure the survival. Another monthly procedure I witnessed was a needle going into her back to drain the cancer fluid from her lungs. I could see her weakness as she breathed. I could see her frustration, having to put herself through such pain, her body weakening. My mom always said, "You don't ask 'why me,' you say, 'why not me'." No one is different or more valuable than the other. My mom truly was her own hero. With such self-love, she never thought she rose above others, especially in God's Graces.

So, the day, that day, I thought she'd bounce back. It was early in the morning. My dad said she's having a hard time breathing, that she needs to go to the hospital. I very quickly arranged care for the kids, and I drove to my parents' place. We were just five minutes away. She was going to be ok. I was just talking to her last night—we discussed me picking up the dress she ordered from Sears for Mother's Day. In fact, I was going to pick the dress up that evening after our call, but she said, "No, tomorrow is fine." That's today, so she will be fine. It's Mother's Day in two days, she'll be fine, I'm getting the dress. We arrived at the house, and the ambulance had just left, and firefighters were coming out of the house.

I ran up the front stairs, silently, but in a fury to see her. The carpets were all moved, and the dining room table was on a slant. This made my stomach turn in knots—my mom taken by ambulance. We must go to the hospital. We get into our minivan, my husband behind the wheel, my dad in the passenger seat. We had taken out our middle seats, so I was way in the back with lots of space between us.

Heart racing, pumping. I said, "Is she ok? Is she getting admitted?"

My dad responded, "They need us for paperwork for your mom."

"Dad, what's going on? Is she ok?"

There was a quiver in his voice. "Your mom is gone."

I blanked and went into complete meltdown. I didn't know I could even experience emotions that would bring me to my knees. But I did, and I haven't really revisited that day until now. As I am writing this, I'm back in the van feeling that girl's pain, more now than ever, even though many years have passed. I was just thirty-two.

I sat with her for hours, just holding her hand, being in the moment. I remember the nurse coming in and handing us string to

loop around her fingers to take off her rings. I knew which one I'd keep—it was the one with pink diamond inside, with diamonds all around.

To her, it symbolized her cancer, in the middle, and her friends and family who were all around her supporting her in the fight. It was hard when they wanted to take her away. I didn't want her to be alone, ever. I didn't want to say goodbye, and I didn't want to lose her touch.

My dad had lost his wife, his companion, his best friend. He gained God's strength. My dad was her saviour through her journey. The man has his wings. He is heaven on earth.

In his Velcro shoes and worn-out work hands, he carried her; it was his footprints in the sand.

It seemed like the whole city showed up the day of my mom's visitation.

My sister and I didn't know whether we would throw up, or cry deliriously, or do them all at the same time—we were all out of sorts. Our mom was gone.

As requested, her music played as we all walked out together.

"River of Dreams"
Written by Billy Joel
In the middle of the night
I go walking in my sleep
Through the valley of fear
To a river so deep
I've been searching for something
Taken out of my soul
Something I'd never lose
Something somebody stole

Our circle is not smaller because she's no longer in it, but bigger and stronger because she was.

In the last year before she passed, my mother wrote my sister and I a book about her life, with personalized inscriptions for each of us. She wrote all about her life, her love and personal messages. Her words are even more impactful when I look back on them.

"Of light for your family and walk the walk to your destiny. I'm always here for you always, my love, my sweet, my destiny, you."

I didn't know it then, but the positive impact of my mom's life would continue to inspire my actions, my words, and my passions.

Chapter 5
Twenty-Four Candles

I was twenty and pregnant with my second child, living in a tiny two-bedroom apartment. My kitchen table was a cheap, plastic patio set with a dollar store fruit tablecloth. I didn't care. I was happy to be in a better place in my life. Yes, I considered this a much happier place from the one I had left, emotionally.

I met my second husband through a mutual friend. He was a hard worker, a stand-up guy—so much so that when I told him I was pregnant on our first date, he said in a comical way, "That's not the best news I've heard all day, but let's go get a movie." He was a comic sometimes, and easy going.

I had a daughter six months later, and a year later we married.

I was probably the only one that day to have two men, past husband and future husband, present in the delivery room as my—our—daughter made her arrival. The nurse turned to me during my first couple of pushes and asked if there were any more men in the hallway. The nurses can suddenly become comedians when you give them material to work with!

Ok. So two dads in delivery, one marriage ending, and a new one beginning.

Here we grow.

What a house! My favourite house, and it became the entertainment house. Over time, we had a movie theatre, pool, darts, a huge jacuzzi bathroom, and a poker table.

I loved being social, and our home was our entertainment in our happy married life—very secure, very loving married life, solid life. We had lawn talks with the neighbours; there were three couples. We would grab our lawn chairs some nights on one of our lawns, and have some alcohol bevies, or in the morning, coffee. Talks "on the stoop" were my favourite with one of my closest neighbours. I played the role of a sister more than a neighbour; that's how close we became. We were each other's rocks; we were each other's constant support, for different reasons, and that would evolve as the years took shape forming our future. And for the same reasons, our conversations would deepen.

I was pregnant with my third child, and our first together—we lost him. Our first-born son. He died the day we met him. Wrapped in a blanket, we held him and held him, knowing we'd have to let him go to his resting place. I have him exactly as I met him embedded in my mind, heart, and soul. I can still smell the hospital-grade blanket he was wrapped in, with his tiny hands curled up under his chin. He was love. He got his wings that day.

We had to endure such pain. We were each other's support for comfort as we were both going through the loss. Four days before my twenty-fifth birthday. There are no words to describe the loss of a child. I was admitted on the maternity floor, and my room was between the rooms of all the new moms with their babies. I soothed myself by talking to the moms as I walked down the halls, the sweet cries of life. They were holding their lambs from God while mine wandered to him.

The day we held him, we lost him.

In in my late thirties, I saw a Reiki energy healer. She said, "There's a little boy saying, 'Don't forget me.' He's always with you."

That day wiped me out—I cried for a day and slept for another.

I was giving my body rest from everything. Days after we lost our son, I started hemorrhaging and had to go back to emergency where they did a a dilation and curettage—a scraping of my uterus. There was a tiny piece of placenta left from the labour and delivery. It was supposed to be a day surgery and go home, but nope—when I was in recovery, I started a high fever and signs of pneumonia. I was admitted for the week. We decided no more children. No more pregnancies. My husband was scheduled for, you know, a snip, snip in the fall months. But six months later, a missed period happened and a pregnancy test was purchased.

I guess God had other plans. He was watching Earth that day and blessed us. Along came another son, completing our family.

We did it. We had so many low and highlighted moments, as the kids grew and we grew—years of diaper changes, car accidents, dance recitals, birthday parties, moving, camping, hockey, broken femurs, and baseball. My mother's death, my grandmother's death, and my aunt's death, and weddings and more funerals. Disney... New York became our second home. Christmas with family, New Year's Eve at Times Square, and Las Vegas, where we renewed our vows fifteen years later in the famous little white chapel, not by Elvis but by Edward Norton and Kristen Wiig look-alikes. I kept thinking, what an odd couple, not knowing in that moment that we, in the future, would become that the odd couple.

I overthink everything. I even overthink overthinking.

When my second marriage ended, I couldn't help but ask myself, "Was it an end, or a pause...?"

It was an ending. We grew. We grew on different paths.

My world—our world—changed, comforts changed, passion, the routine changed. One minute you're waking up like Phil and Claire and living *The Modern Family* life, and in a blink, you wake up like Will and Grace—roommates and sarcasm—and then to the couple from *The Break-Up* with Vince Vaughn and Jennifer Aniston. Emotions raw, until the place that once felt like home and full of life and love was now cold, bare, sad, quiet, and mute.

My daughter was at college, my oldest was. working full time, and our son was just sixteen. So extremely sad. No one wins in separation—no ribbons, just papers.

Living an authentic life came at the price of ending a marriage. No matter the time invested, the time you invest in yourself is more important. It does make me feel sad for those two people who, so grounded by morals and a healthy environment for their family, grew apart.

Months later I moved into my dad's house, this time knowing a little bit more of my value, more mental strength, to know my worth.

During my first marriage, I didn't hold myself accountable.

My second marriage, I did—we both did. Neither of us wanted to put in the fight. Clearly, when your husband turns to you and says, "I hate that pink lipstick," which, by the way, I had been wearing every day for… forever. We weren't trying. Well, actions and words that night told me all I needed to know.

We deserved more than we were giving to each other.

Chapter 6
Taste of Local

Coffee, a warm hug. My day started with filling a cup of a hug with cream and sugar, of course. Coffee: the wake-me-up, shake-me-up drink of choice. All day! Yes, I like it almost as much as the name for my ideas.

I have a name for my ideas, my entrepreneur moments of ideas, the thunder of ideas comes in light: a camera flash. They seem to just slowly wave in, just as I process my thought, and the wave of ideas flows, and then like a camera, the vision is exposed. They always remained in sheet lightening mode. Lying flat. Oh, I would process each idea, believe me; I even tried to bring them up in conversation with others. I just never got those pictures developed.

I can hear your thoughts as you read—you're interested to know one. Well, one was called Pillow Talk, and again, I hear your pause... Pillow Talk was an idea, a cushioned idea, of a store with all pillows—accessory pillows, bed pillows, and yes, pillow covers, a real cloud nine when your head hit the pillow. That idea went to the clouds and never came back down. Not in our financial cards.

As I'm taking in the warm hug of coffee, I turn on the TV on Netflix, of course. It was on the home screen, and *Shopaholic* was in my Watch Again list. My TV was on top of my dresser, angled toward the bed, my closets behind. I was working at a local car dealership my mom retired from because of her cancer. The owners offered me position there, as I was on a leave from managing a McDonald's at night. The owners approached me at my mother's funeral. They were like brothers. She worked there for eleven years. I took them up on their offer. I was there eight years, working in the office. I did sales, too, but I loved being in the office. So many jobs to do, it was endless. For someone like me, I needed that "busy." So, you can imagine my wardrobe after eight years and countless trips to New York. I had quite the wardrobe, a closet store, if you will. It was *Shopaholic* on the TV and in the closet behind it. That day helped me decide my future without realizing it at the time. Thank you, Sophie Kinsella, for that camera flash of inspiration.

I'm going to have a clothing sale this weekend, but not just any sale, a community sale. I will open it up to the public, and I will make it boutique style, and so on and so on; my brain started a wave, a lightening wave. A camera flash this time would develop, my idea would grab hold and grow with each thought, rippling into more.

Let's begin. First things first—we get to work. By we, I mean anyone I could get to donate. It's a Sunday, so I start cleaning my closets, and pour more coffee. Through the week, between work and preparing for this fundraiser,

I managed to pull a community of friends and neighbours and coworkers to join in, feel the positive impact, and make a difference in the lives of others battling cancer in our community.

Usually, it's just the clinics or research we gather to donate to; they're the usual recipients of the monetary donations. I feel that it's important to bring a bright spot to the patients. Why can't we do both, donate to the clinic and its patients? Everyone was on board, and we were executing the plan.

I couldn't be more excited for this sale. I even set it up like a store and thought, why not use the big painted chalkboard wall so the guest shoppers could sign to show they supported the cause. I could take a picture, and when I dropped off the donation, I could include the picture of the chalkboard wall.

What a success, what a weekend. A labour of love, what a calling.

The whole community came together for The Closet Sale, and we were able to gift a donation to the cancer care clinic and gifts to cancer care patients. This was a tribute to my mom, in her honour.

I was approached days later by the owner of a local tackle shop. He was holding the same vision, which he believed could become something the public would want to be a part of—a continuous journey to donate to cancer patients. His wife had passed away one year prior; that was his "why." I said "yes," left my full-time job, and tackled the 200 square foot rental space. I cashed in my RRSP and invested it into the little closet that could.

The passion had to have meaning, and the community had to be a part of it.

The name would have to make sense and be simple. Everyone had one and donated from "The Closet Door." The colours were black and white, the colours of the chalk and chalkboard.

I had a goal, more than a business plan. I had a chalkboard, chalk, in-style donated clothing, and a space. A home doesn't have a business plan—it has love. Love evolved as I grew. Heart hugs became a constant in the Closet. I saw the vision in the camera flash and started to develop it. I put everything I had into it.

The Closet Door would be in honour of my mom. A space where people would come together for a cause. To gift cancer care patients, like she gifted to those close to her, and those who impacted her life. Gifting was a part of her life. I will always remember her gifting a nurse who was new and just coming into her caring career. She would hand out coffee gift cards to some of her fellow patients as they were receiving treatments. When I took leave from my job, she had me continue to drop off coffees and cookies to her co-workers at the car dealership when she was too weak to do it herself. I felt her when I gifted. It was our hands reaching others'.

The true story behind The Closet Door: the healing would be greater than the cause. It would impact everyone in the community that it touched. It would be a true passion, staffed by volunteers selling in-style donated clothing for a cause, wearing our hearts on our sleeves. The clothing donations would come from community members from all walks of life, as would the shoppers. Everyone who donated clothing or shopped would sign their name to "The Chalkboard of Supporters." It would truly be a community labour of love.

Oh, I know some probably thought it might not become what it is today. I knew what it could be, but my "why" would make it possible, my passion would be its strength. I didn't want words of uncertainty to dim the vision; I wanted to show them its light. Don't leave before the magic, stay to see it happen.

We installed a wall-size chalkboard so everyone could leave their mark. My dad made the chalkboard, so it meant just a little bit more. We opened on May 11th, the anniversary of my mom's passing.

The chalkboard and chalk took on a whole new meaning.

I can't tell you the feeling of all the love in that space, but I can tell you I wanted the world to feel more of it. We were building momentum gifting cancer care patients with the proceeds monthly. The store was expanding to a new location. I needed help. I would need to have all hands-on deck, more kind hands.

Soon I had two volunteers, and as we grew, in time, my Closet Squad family evolved.

The Closet Door became a household name around our community.

Closet Love surrounded us all.

We slowly started to make it the biggest walk-in closet for a cause. We were closed Sunday and Mondays to give us time to stock, sort, and find creative closet ways to keep improving our shopping flow.

One Sunday, there was a knock on the door. It was a lady, not just any lady but a stylist for a play showcasing at our local theatre. We had just got in a line of vintage clothing. She had heard about us, and purchased the vintage collection, all while donating to the cause. Lights and camera flash, and the thunder rolled. It turned out that one of the cast members was local and wanted to volunteer. Together, the idea of events rippled through our minds.

The wave kept going and we created so many super events. Fashion shows with skits to music, "Loonie-Toonie" auctions, a Broadway Show called "Chalk," trivia nights, local artists in a song writers' circle. Each event was sold out.

By the time we opened our third location, I had over twenty volunteers, and we introduced refurbished furniture pieces that the community donated. I would tag each furniture piece with the name of the person who donated it to the cause. Everyone was a part of The Closet Door, no matter what. Everyone got their name on the chalkboard. After making countless wishes and monetary donations to our local cancer care clinic, our name is forever engraved on the local hospital donation board. Together we have impacted many lives, our own included. The hospital foundation and the love and care of the cancer care clinic nursing staff was the icing on the cake for all who ran it. I was blessed to be able to give shape to CAKE.

I will forever be grateful for the unconditional love, the warmth of The Closet, and those who, with grace, gave their kind hands and warm hearts. I met my very best friend inside The Closet Door. Together we grew events and stood together on life's changing platform, the stage.

Hosting, developing new ideas, an investment he made into this closet. My world is priceless. I welcomed more family into my heart. As I have given by opening The Closet Door, my mom left the gift of Closet love. The most valuable and unselfish love comes from within The Closet Door.

In the years that follow, I was given the kindness award, and named the hometown hero. What a humbling and positive moment, to find comfort in the cause, to know we had helped patients fight through their cancer by bringing a bright light of wishes granted. The cause, as it was always meant to be, more than anything, a human touch.

I was also a part of a tribute over the holiday season. The hospital had many strands of blue lights to honour the donors. My sister's words sent such love and warmth to my heart, as she said with love:

"I'd like to think that each bulb on those strands of life represents a life that you added a little light to because of your generosity over the years."

"It takes a community to build a closet."

Closet love surrounded us. We developed lifelong friendships, and each learned who we were—we gained our own identities. It helped us to root and evolve ourselves and each other in compassion, strength, relationships, respect, and gain confidence for what world lies ahead for us. It gave us the tools to become best versions of ourselves. More chairs at my table.

Be a door opener.

Be with purpose.

Be love.

Be you.

Chapter 7
CAKE Smash

Cancer affects us all and we can all have an effect. The Closet Door grew from passions. It grew because I had angel volunteers. It grew from community kindness, and it grew beyond the doors of the brick and mortar.

The first event drew interest from the community who shopped for a cause. I choreographed a fashion show—not runway style but more of a skit to music style. The volunteers acted out the closet door with its purpose. All proceeds gifted to patients and a donation to the clinic.

I sold tickets, had rehearsals, and invited local vendors.

The day came and my anxiety set in. Who would really be coming? Did the community just buy tickets to support, or did they see my value of fundraising outside the walls? Would they show?

The photographer was the first to show up, then the vendors. The volunteers scurried to the makeshift dressing room where the clothing I had all numbered and for the various skits were waiting. Guests started to arrive, one by one by one, with my family in the front row. After I posed for some photo opportunities backstage, I came out to see how many guests had arrived. It was packed, with standing room only. It was in that moment, I felt overwhelmed. My labour of love, my camera flash, my trust in the process, was happening, and people saw and believed in its light, believed in my passion, and were on board to see the magic. This event was just the beginning of a legacy, driven by one girl who gifted a positive impact, and who inspired a community of love.

Happiness is an inside job. The Closet Door was filled with volunteers who gifted more than just their time. They also gifted from their hearts. All the volunteers had their own personal "whys," and they all had been affected by cancer on some level. We created a video to showcase the meaning behind their decisions to gift time. My best friend directed and filmed it. This was reflected in one of the reviews posted to The Closet Doors Facebook page:

"Never have I seen people give so much of themselves and dedicate their time to a cause as much as these people do."

They are all my forever family.

The events grew, and my community partnerships and relationships grew too. In the beginning, I was the only one propelling The Closet Door. I knew how hard it was to foster relationships with others to expand its meaning and who I was. So as The Closet Door became a part of the community, and people connected with me on a level of someone who was inspiring, I started to venture out supporting other new local businesses, and the community followed.

Together we would create bigger events that would bring an even greater impact.

My first community partnership event had the mission of granting wishes to Cancer Care patients. The partnership was with my best friend and his real estate team, headed by a man who wanted to support local. It was a sold-out New Year's Eve ticketed event for the community to attend. I placed a wish box at The Cancer Care Clinic so that the patients as they received treatments could fill out their wishes. That event was not only a huge success, but our mission was more of a success: all of the wishes were granted. Through the years to this day, we still continue events together beyond the brick and mortar and supporting various causes in our community. A caring crew, all hands-on deck, always, with love.

I became so invested, reaching more, supporting more than the cancer care in my community. The Closet Door hosted exclusive shopping nights for the LGBTQ2S+ community. I began to be approached to host events that supported Heart and Stroke, local networking groups, talent shows, and music festivals. My role extended from just The Closet Door Lady. I felt my passions in all levels supporting my community.

In everything I do it is with ethics, love, passion and kindness. I was nominated by the community for a Hometown Hero Award and was one of four recipients in southern Ontario that year. My best friend and I were the first to receive Freedom House's Kindness Award, humbled, a true honor. We do what we do because we want to, not for any other reason. I didn't even know there was such an award for being a human being. Kind attracts kindness.

The cause didn't close because the doors did. It did the opposite—opening up to continue, beyond the brick and mortar, knowing the camera flash did more than develop. It processed and came to full exposure to the world.

It truly is a CAKE smash.

Chapter 8
Chalk-late Cake

The Closet Door is an extension of me, and my mom and all those apart of it with authentic and kind hearts. Closing the door on the last day, I took a chair and just stared at "The Chalkboard of Supporters." All the names that blessed its cause and my life. The chalkboard was a huge part, and it set us aside from any other business because it was run by the hearts of community. I didn't do it alone. I always said I am the director, and the community are the producers, and together we're making a lifetime movie. Everyone has a part.

No one will truly know the deep love I have for The Closet Door.

The Closet Door was home. It will always be a part of me. You can take the girl out of the closet, but you can't take the closet out of the girl. The moments, the community, the volunteers, my family, is its heartbeat. It truly was the little closet that could and did.

One event honouring my mom was a Loonie-Toonie auction fundraiser held on May 11th, the anniversary of her passing. In her honour, I asked my musician friend to play "River of Dreams" by Billy Joel, which had been so meaningful to her during her treatments, and so meaningful to us when it was performed at her funeral. He learned it for us and performed it at our event in her honour. This, with the abundance of love and support in the room made the event that more meaningful. My mom's memory and legacy lives on, through all that knew her, through our gifting, and that day, through song. Years later another musician friend wrote a song telling the story of The Closet Door. She performed it at a songwriter's circle that my best friend and I organized and hosted together in honour of The Closet Door.

Both these artists shared their gift of music for the cause, and felt the passion for it, authentically. They are rock stars.

My mom was always sharing herself with us. One Christmas she surprised us with a song that she had written herself, "Masterpiece." She had written it and had a singer record it on a cassette for me and my sister, just after her mom passed. Her words, the lyrics of her song, left an imprint. An imprint like the memorably drawn heart she used to sign her name with. My daughter and I now wear it proudly as a tattoo like a "heart on our sleeve." We imprinted ourselves with her, like she imprinted on us. Carrying her with us, always. I have always gone back to those lyrics as a comfort, back to the meaning behind the words.

"Masterpiece" lyrics

"You are a lamb of God, you are a masterpiece,

a new creation he has formed, and you're as soft and fresh as a snowy winter morn, and I'm so glad that God has given you to me, little lamb of God, you are a masterpiece."

I felt those words on that day in the hospital after losing our son.

And again, on the day we lost our mom.

Mom, you are a Masterpiece.

Gifting hands never goes out of style and truly is priceless.

Everything happens for a reason, and I truly believe that we were all destined to meet in the closet. It was triumph over tragedy. It was where relationships developed, lifetime moments enriched from its positive impacts, and fuel for growth.

It takes one person to bring change and takes a village to bring its waters to ripples when the waves touch it.

I am proud and I am humbled. I am touched by my community of heart. Every month it rained true from all those who signed their name to the chalkboard, proof that The Closet Door was a triumph.

The writing is on the wall, as they say.

The chalkboard may not be on the wall in a physical sense, but the names still hold its value in my heart.

Chalk didn't just leave a mark on the Chalkboard

It changed me, it shaped me, it stood by me, and it showed me the magic…

…like I knew it would.

Chapter 9
Takes the CAKE

"When one door closes, another one opens."

—Alexander Graham Bell.

The Closet Door, as much as it brought passion and positive impact, my personal life took to thunder and life's downpour, but there were also beautiful moments to light the storm—learning self-care and how to lean on others. Through the seven years that The Closet Door operated as a bricks and mortar location, a lot had happened: I had to close and reopen at three different locations, pauses of life on hold, my marriage ending, financial impacts, working in between jobs, my nan dying, a failed and toxic short-lived relationship, and moved into the basement of my uncle's bungalow again. Starting from the ground up. The final closure of my store. My sister moved away. A cancer scare. Becoming caregiver to a family member.

I provided support to friends, and, at times, I was drowning. And at those times of wanting to throw in the towel, I turned my anxiety into positive passion and said "One more time" at each storm. Just one more time. "Life is a marathon not a sprint," Dr. Phil once said. The man who said that to me one time, he himself took his marathon, and filled the track with his own camera flash into the future. He built his real estate team; he continues running. I took that advice and my own, tied my shoes started to walk, and with each day began to run again. Put my life back on track—at my own pace.

Thank-you for the happiest years of my life.

As I began to close the doors to the store for the last time because the owner was selling, I was painting over the names on the chalkboard. I would never erase the names. It's good karma to have them layered through the paint, then covered. That moment, painting over them, I had a thought, a light of the camera flash for my next business. Clean Slate.

It would be a clean slate in my career path and in my personal path. I would partner with a childhood friend. She was an anchor at one of life's difficult moments. A saviour.

The new door opened to real estate cleans and commercial cleans. And now instead of coming into my closet, I'd be coming to yours, in a matter of speaking.

My passions would continue beyond the bricks and mortar. I can't stop. I won't stop.

Gifting my life, literally, will continue to gift cancer care.

Chapter 10
Single Slice

I am not going to do it, nope. Not me, I couldn't… but what if? So, I did. I plunged into online dating—I barely even got my toes wet. But I did wear a life jacket.

It's a lot of work setting up a dating profile.

First, which dating apps are deemed the safest? Which picture to use? Honesty is the best policy; honesty in what you are looking for. You're basically writing a resume; your life experiences are your history—without references. I'd say, add the reference part; it would help.

I came to find that not everyone is who they say they are, and pictures only reveal the surface, not the truth. Have them take a selfie with your name on a piece of paper and send you the photo. This prevents catfishing.

You try different avenues; you become a detective and search them on social media and Instagram before feeling or giving them any kind of interest. Be guarded through these investigations. Being in their company—in person—helps a lot more.

Sometimes online dating looks as if rows of chairs are lined up on either side of a hallway. All of us single women are sitting, waiting to hold a conversation with a match. Sometimes your name is called, sometimes it's not, and sometimes you make a bowl of popcorn during long pauses in-between (I like to call that intermission). My absolute favourite. Not so much, but the popcorn is good. I add Smarties to it.

My safe word is "Tippy Toe." Feel free to use that as well! It's safe! It works; I only ever had to use it once.

Like anything else, single life lessons are best when we live them through experiences and growth, and I grew and outgrew this stage quickly.

Like the fast and furious. Some dates gone in sixty seconds. Break out the Crest 3D white and make them smile. Coffee shops are safe and public, and if I can't enjoy the date, I can enjoy my bevy, and refill for dates ahead.

Ghosting is when someone disappears from the conversation page, with no warning, not even a goodbye—poof. I can tell you, the person behind the picture or messages feels it and it stings.

That's sometimes how the CAKE crumbles.

Chapter 11
Cup-CAKE

So, you cast your single line and a lot of the time you release after a few minutes, because they don't message you, or simply because they took your line while taking others at the same time.

We were taught not to talk to strangers, yet here we are…

… talking to strangers.

Dating is like an online catalogue, and sometimes it's like in the fairy tale—holding a ball and trying to find the right prince or princess. Sometimes I think kissing a frog would be better.

Our fuel tank becomes empty. I felt I had to keep the search going, and I do, because I believe my match is out there. I even researched the sites for success stories; there were some, which helped me to believe it could happen to me… proof that it did happen to others.

When I started, I realized that whatever stage you're on, make sure that person is standing beside you, and will pass you the mic.

Have a clear mind, an open mind, because your soul mate is you. The happiness you want to share with someone, be the first to give it to yourself. The moments and wants from someone will be received at a calmer pace if you first fuel yourself. When you are fully fueled, that's when you can give fuel gracefully, with love, and without giving it all at once.

Here's the reality, though; everyone's at a different stage in life. They are saying everything you want to hear, and then realizing that they don't even have a toe in the same stage as you. You can't manufacture love; you cannot settle for anything less. Don't waste your time or give more of yourself in the first intro, less is more. Time can't be measured by success. Be patient.

On the hamster wheel of dating, you have chosen truly what you want and need. Let the good times roll, wink. I sometimes take a pause, sit in the hamster wheel, close the door, grab snacks, and binge Netflix shows.

Some date night suggestions: make sure you take the sticker off the new jeans you just bought—trust me, it's happened. You know, that long sticker that runs down the back of the leg. Or keep it; it could make for a great conversation piece.

Honestly, I have yet to crack the code on modern-day dating. If I did, I'd already have a number one best seller.

I have come to realize this so far through my conversations with men and their perceptions, and of course, with mine.

Women's search seems to be focussed on men's height. Men want the focus on their toys (trucks, ATVs, boats, motorcycles) and fish. Do men want woman to think they are the catch of the day? It's funny how we really haven't changed in some respects from our child-like focus. Little girls want someone to look up to. As a little boy, so proud of their Hot Wheels collection, and the catch of their first fish. Somethings just grow and stay with us.

It doesn't matter if the man and woman have mutual friends; it doesn't matter the city they live in, their age, their interests, the material items they own, their house, their profile, their job, the size of the fish they caught, their beliefs—everything looks great on paper. It happens in the moment; in-person is the true test, if you get it. It is then the pilot light ignites and glows a bit brighter for some, and while for others, it goes out. Be aware of "red flags", but don't be blind to the "green flags."

Keep moving in this slice of life. Don't take it personally.

Secretly, though not so secret now, I want to just live in the moment and message them, "I like you, let's go grab food. I have Big Mac coupons, what do you say?" I think they will bite!

Or perhaps…

… just a cup of coffee, to find the connection.

Chapter 12
Coffee CAKE

The place where friends go to be friends; it's-not-you-it's-me zone. I'm-just-not-ready zone and you're-too-nice zone.

I found more than half the time, I felt like I sat on most dates as a therapist into their own searches and past relationships. Some still talk about their exes as if they were in the now and not the ex. I did have patience and I try to be always kind, even if I know… No.

I was cupid to many—just a hard time to match me, myself, and I.

I matched with some who were in the beginning of online dating, and I matched with some that were just on a different stage but were friendly enough to come honestly to that conclusion. Years later, they would swipe on my profile just so that they could peek in, making sure I was doing well, and life was kind in the dating world. It felt like there was a group beneath it all. I call it the "SS group"— Still Single.

Wherever I go, whatever I do, I always end up making friends. My best friend often says to those who come into my path, "Once you meet her, you'll have a friend for life."

I got a camera flash while dating. I can see an idea develop. My target audience would be the town singles.

Allow me to explain: You're dating, and you go into their bathroom and see personalized towels. Instead of "his" and "hers," they say, "his" and "could be yours." Ahh… a match made in heaven. I'll pin it for now—it's a great gift idea. It would be fun as a new up-and-coming relationship evolves to see this when you use their bathroom.

This idea is in the dark room developing, and maybe will one day,

will see the light.

On my "circle of dating life," I did meet the sweetest gentle soul, his demeanour kind, just as much as his smile. We sat for an afternoon having coffee, cake, and refills. He was a true gentleman, but his personality was quite shy; he sometimes couldn't look at me when he replied. We had a light flow of conversation that was more focused on how he could come out of his shell to have comfort in dating.

I tried the best I could to help with his process, as I too felt this way in the beginning of dating. It can be intimidating at first, to say the least. We met because I looked familiar, and he messaged me on Messenger, or "slid into my DMs," as they say, because he looked familiar from my high school days.

He messaged me weeks later to thank me, and we joked that I could be his wing woman; you never know whose life you'll change. Always be kind. Always make the time to hear people's voices.

It's human kindness.

I know now online dating isn't for me. I couldn't tell sometimes if I was serving my purpose or just theirs. I could feel my fuel burning low. I needed to trust the process. I used to say in some conversations with matches, I was going to call Elon Musk to put me in one of his rockets and take me to Mars to see their leader. Then, I'd match him with our leader on Venus. The dating world saved!

They would laugh. I would laugh.

I am aware there are lots of men out there, but I'm searching for one man, my man. And I didn't see him online. I have gone through all the apps in all the land, and he wasn't there.

God gives us the opportunity.

Online dating was one opportunity; each swipe is an opportunity to meet, and each date is an opportunity to build.

I don't just want that slice of opportunity; I want the whole damn CAKE.

Chapter 13
CAKE Tiers

I had a few relationships after my second marriage ended.

Looking back, as I write this from the present, I didn't need someone to just hold my cup, I needed them to help fill it. I know that now.

Slow and steady does win the race, because if we don't go slow, it trips us up. I started to create so much love for the two of us. I fueled these relationships by fueling both of us. I felt enriched in the love that I composed, and I was expecting so little. That is what I got. I was fueled by empty actions.

There were some of the most amazing moments in the beginning and the middle, where I made choices based on facts, which I vocalized. I was fueling relationships that had a hole in the bottom and no matter how much I gave to patch the holes; it wasn't enough to stay afloat. In the end, it sank. We sank. Yes, we had our ups and downs.

What we need. What we gain. What we lose. Life is always shaping us to become our greatest selves, if that's what we want. If we don't, we settle only into disappointment and guilt. The guilt of not living our full potential and finding that balance. To make a life with someone is to find a balance—meet me halfway.

My mistake was that I started being the girlfriend before I was ever the girlfriend.

It felt like being at the water park—fun, right? At first, your excitement builds, you're confident you're going to have fun. Until you get to this moment, not realizing you're standing under the big bucket until you look up and see it slowly filling with water—the stress, the anxiety—knowing it would release the heaviness of it all on you.

Then it repeats. You feel paralyzed and alone, standing under it, while you watch your partner just standing off to the side watching you. That's what I feel when I'm left unloved, carrying the weight of the negativity, the mocking, the sarcasm, the taunting, the projecting, the tension, the downpour, and all I want is to leave.

I wished, just once, they would have held the umbrella, so we could weather the storm together. I forgave myself for allowing men to treat me this way. The forgiveness allowed me, each time, to make me a stronger version of myself. I forgave myself for not seeing my value. We are all human. We need to forgive, be kind to ourselves. We need to end the cycle. Self-love is love. Don't leave your faucet to drip, and don't carry the buckets of the load of the relationship, especially with a hole in the bucket.

"You can close your eyes to the things you don't want to see, but you can't close your heart to things you don't want to feel"

CAKE

—Johnny Depp

Trust in whatever process heals you, helps you thrive, and tests your ultimate limits, especially in your relationship.

Cut a slice for you first.

Chapter 14
Patty CAKE,
Patty CAKE

The walls we build—well, there's a reason for that.

I hear people all the time; they say, don't keep your wall up, show who you are to people, so they know all about you—no secrets. All cards on the table.

You cannot grow a relationship on your own; when you meet someone, you want to grow together. In my experience, you tend to be co-dependent very fast if you're both throwing in all your bricks.

I've been there and we attract what we give. If we give all our bricks all at once, where's the build, the balance that both of you will receive? Also, if you only have a short-lived relationship, do you want that person to have all the pieces of you? Your life is yours; own every brick.

Everyone is different, so no two relationships will be the same.

If I'm dating someone, I don't need to be dating their ex through the first moments of our conversation, or what their ex was like, beyond just their relationship—my personality may be different. My relationship is intimate, private, and personal, and I would not want to awaken in someone else's (my exes') new relationship. I have my story; let me tell it, not them. Let me hold onto those moments and allow myself to grow gracefully in a new relationship.

The bricks are very important, not only to share with others, but each one tells a story, a moment, a relationship, friends, your emotions, your health, your image, your self-worth, your memories, your education, your work experiences, your likes and dislikes, your childhood. All have been placed, in order, from the ground up. Do you see all the value in these bricks, your bricks?

In the beginning, share a coffee, without spilling the beans.

Chapter 15
CAKE Bites

I wanted to touch base with you about social networks; let's start with Facebook. We are all in control of our walls. Again, the bricks are all down for some, while others are placed one brick at a time. It's a peek into our lives, but we are in control of how much we allow others into our world. I use it as a platform to help bring awareness to the community and support local; I share a brick one at a time. I also include the fun and open side of me. I have a circle of friends who support me. Some may not have a support system, so their bricks are all out. They need their Facebook circle to support, to listen.

Facebook is their platform, their therapy, their one and only social circle. That's ok; it's their wall, it's their platform. But they also must survive in a world of trolls—those who could use their sensitivity and take the situation for granted. It's a curse and a blessing. Be aware; it is a reality that wolves in sheep's clothing also have the ability to be invited in.

Facebook is like a reality show, except without the script, without the rose at the end, or the sweepstakes.

It's a spider web that weaves us all together, and just as quickly sweeps us apart.

It's a curse and a blessing. I am a people person; I love connecting with what fuels me.

I love the feel-good parts, and I appreciate the hearts and souls that people put out, and of course, any pickle recipes and coffee memes.

We never know what other people are going through.

That's another reason why I am writing this book. So many can relate to a similar experience; hopefully it will help someone.

Facebook is and has been a great tool for connecting the community, especially when, in its good graces, it allowed me to spread my business and my passions to donate to cancer care. I used the print form, too, connecting through a newspaper, but Facebook helped my message spread farther than just my community. Positive impact, a blessing in that all walks of life were brought together... it should be called Face-lives.

Here I am writing away, but the world has gone into a pandemic and the world has gone and got sick.

"When life hands you lemons..." In this case, well, it handed the world a whole case of lemons.

Yes, the world got sick and put us all in a mental, physical, and emotional house arrest.

Nobody knows what's going on, but there's fear of the unknown; Facebook and Instagram are on overdrive, and

TikTok-mania was about to explode as entertainment of the year. People of the world now saw themselves as stars.

Covid-19, millions of lives lost, the daily death tolls are rising, hospitals are full, our loved ones are all divided. We are isolated in our homes. We are running out for necessities, trying to get masks, everything is selling out, we don't know how long the world will be shut down, our carts are full, overflowing, we can't seem to get enough in it, or even think. Over just a few days, shelves are empty, toilet paper and paper towel are sold out, shelves are bare, so I start buying boxes of Kleenex—I mean, it's better than nothing. All necessities, including baking essentials, are gone. We were not prepared. I even bought a couple of turkeys, as meat was selling fast. Panic set in, and at best, we felt that we were on a show where we had a minute to grab and go. I think I did it in thirty seconds. They say a little laughter helps, but honestly the smiles were miles away, hidden under our mandatory masks.

It was a surreal moment for all of us. It changed us all. Everything felt longer. And heavy. Businesses closed, families separated, and dating? No way! We were all on lockdown, restricted to our homes. I was grateful to be living with my uncle and dad, but I couldn't spend time with my kids or sister and brother-in-law—the virus was so widespread.

As this progressed into three major lockdowns and the government is calling for a fourth, we are all living this. As you read this, no matter what this is, it's something we are all enduring. Life is incredibly hard right now; we are all just trying to live in a world together, grasping at the good, trusting in the process. I don't have all the answers, but I have faith there are better days ahead.

There is confusion about this pandemic, certain restrictions not making sense, people united and while others are divided on the government trying to make us all get "the Vax"—that's what we call it. Two shots a month apart to reduce the virus attacking us fully, and having our bodies surrendered to a hospital bed, on a ventilator, to possibly death.

Some viewed this as a conspiracy, some thought it was to just be a flu virus, and some thought it was manmade. It was hard to see the future without masks, without debate, without deaths, and without restrictions. We are the world; we make it go around, and when it stopped, we kept going. Some went in different directions, some in the same, but we kept going.

I am one to make every day a production, a stage to grab life's ladder and keep going. Sometimes I trip, lose my footing, but I always keep going. Appreciate my single life, embrace it, have faith, and make good choices.

We all create different Band-Aids for ourselves. I call them Band-Aids because it's all temporary—moments, people, situations. Slowly the Band-Aids will fall off naturally after the healing.

…don't rip off the Band-Aid, before you heal.

Chapter 16
40ish Candles

This is forty-ish. I'll be honest; it gets real. "I'm coming in HOT!" It's almost as if a door pops up with a sign that reads, "This Way," and you walk through a calmer hallway, some layers peeling away like an onion, the core underneath the layers—these are the best parts of yourself.

Being forty is fueling, high energy, following life quotes, or TikTok videos, investing in scented candles with labels that match the room decor. It's reading daily horoscopes and feeling at the top of your game, like you have finally come into a little wisdom at this point in your life. Now being forty and single, your bladder goes from a big sponge to a Q-tip size, a pair of glasses at each corner of the house. The meaning of life now is that you remembered to get the coffee prepped the night before.

You feel like God came and took the backpack off your shoulders—the heaviness from holding onto the past, the blessing and release of friendships and said, "Now that should feel lighter."

Everything seems to taste better, especially coffee, I'm a newbie to iced coffee. I see a lot more at this stage of life with open eyes, and I have a lot more patience. Emphasis on a *lot* more.

It feels like at this age there's a lot more to think about. The Bucket List now becomes the To-Do-List and the Not-To-Do-List. Like a woman feels when the clock's ticking to have babies or wondering if she's missed the boat on love. Let me tell you: the sea may be a little rough at times; keep rowing. If we were at sea, you'd see a lot of us out here. Life jackets and coffee and struggling to find bars for our phone.

Life can deflate us, tricks us, trips us.

I've learned the best thing to do is grab your best outfit—you have total control over you. For instance, I am dressed up today. It's a Friday, my day off. I decided to "pump and polish." That's the name I use when getting lashes and nails done. It's the little things I do for me. I take myself out for overpriced coffee and sit with my laptop sharing the day with all of you, as I write. The crowd's good, and this iced coffee is like a spa day, refreshing and good for the soul. Life at forty can be flirty and free.

Remember to make way for all the good. If you're holding on to all the bad, the messy, you can't catch the good because your hands are full. Plus, you still need a hand free for coffee.

Forty-ish is about comfy, cozy, clap-on light dimmers, Alexa, binge-watching Netflix, googling information because who doesn't need to know how old Betty White was when she started *Golden Girls*, or how many organs in a woman's body (I spelled it wrong in the search. It came up five. If you know, you know, lol). It's finding the most comfortable blankets, going down the rabbit hole of Facebook, then coming up for online purchases, leading you down a rabbit hole of things they recommend you buy.

TikToks that hypnotize you, drawing your eyes and mind in. Viewing everything from make-up tutorials, household tricks (because who doesn't need to see all the solutions to keep your toilet bowl clean, or how to make one shirt into twenty different styles). Copious numbers of couples doing flexible moves intertwined like they are trying out for spots on Cirque du Soleil. I found it interesting: when watching a lumberjack show his twig huts while playing on a homemade "handpan" drum, I wondered how they have wi-fi out there to make these and upload them. Perhaps a nearby coffeehouse? TikTok is certainly entertainment, especially for night owls like me. I will use this platform one day, but definitely not to showcase my Cirque du Soleil moves, not quite yet (insert laugh emoji).

Forty is about standing dedicated to your missions. I'm talking about standing in line at Bath & Body Works and decorating with HomeSense, keeping up with the newest Rae Dunn pottery pieces, car maintenance, resetting your fire stick, at-home facials, racing through grocery stores and not checking your list because you think you have it all memorized when you know you never do. It's troubleshooting yourself through solutions, it's making inspirational selfies on social media. Rae Dunn, if you're reading this, you're welcome. That's what I call my "mug shots"!

Right now, I've had cravings for chocolate and dill pickle chips—these are my guilty pleasure. It's late nights in a cozy blanket with the best snacks bedside me, because I can.

You never know how life will unfold. If I could say one, ok, maybe two things to my past self, they would be, "I'll be proud of you" and "learn to lean." It took me until I reached forty to would allow myself the breathing room and mind space emotionally to lean on others for support. Exposing my vulnerabilities, all of me.

I was that person that was the concrete holding others together, but like all concrete it starts to crack, and that's what was happening to me—thin cracks to my mind, body, and soul. I grabbed my life jacket and my paddles and brought some friends with me to help row.

You want to know the truth…?

… I laugh harder with myself; I feel more myself when I am in my own company, and I am taking care of myself more than ever.

I didn't think at forty that I would be living at my uncle's, making a home in his basement apartment, but I understand that this doesn't define me. It protects me, in the present. Grateful for my uncle, for his human kindness; he truly is great.

To move forward, I need to get all my ducks in a row, and not quack up. I had strength, set some goals. I went from running a store, closing a store, a relationship ending, starting completely over. I lost a lot. But in the words of my uncle, it was a perfect storm. Sometimes our losses are our greatest gains.

As I continue to write this two years later (by the way, I haven't a clue about the whole system of writing and publishing, but I'll get there), I am proud of myself; I didn't come this far to only come this far.

Very few knew what was happening behind the scenes. My concrete cracks, filled with blessings, strength and kindness, and coffee. I am a "human bean," roasted to be bold.

… I also light my candle with a picture of Jesus. My Jesus candle. Let me tell you, he can light up a room. Amen.

Almost three years later, after The Closet Door closed its doors, my cleaning business has opened successfully. I'm stronger and wiser now, and can choose who and what surround me. I'm building adult relationships with my daughter and my two sons, with thoughts of my little lamb who wanders in my thoughts.

I spent too much fuel on others, hoping to help them, aid them, fix them, while I used a Band-Aid to cover the surface of my own insecurities. You cannot expect people to change or react the way you would; that only leads to your disappointment.

Slowly, while in my forties and through years of self-reflecting and writing, I finally reached a place in my soul so I can be alone, and it felt calm. My bed saw enough of me, and one day it said, "get up and blow the stink off you," in a matter of speaking.

The road can get rocky, so I got a CAA membership. CAA is definitely one of the best investments. It's in the same hierarchy of best inventions like the Shoppers points card, the Tim Horton's rewards card, fire sticks, and weighted blankets that helps you take some comfort in being single. Thank god for Alexa and her jokes and for putting up with all my questions (I'm surprised she hasn't shut down and put herself on sleep mode, to be honest). Then there's cell phones, data plans (you're not paying $.10 per text; remember those days?) and, and, and… all of the apps in all of the land.

I do have a great idea for a dating app, camera flash idea, and you know what that means.

It may just come to develop.

Say cheese… CAKE!

Chapter 17
CAKE for Breakfast

Cake tastes so much better in your forties; I could eat cake for breakfast. It's fine—it has eggs in it. So, technically it's Egg Cake. Cakes are ever so sweet and are probably everyone's favourite food.

So many choices, options, icing—the icing on my CAKE, is all the sweet people in my life, who have layered their kindness between the cake layers. Then the ones who surround the cake with icing roses, like my Closet Door family; they are the ones that take the cake. These compliment your tastes, give you that excitement, that sweet rush and that glow, the candle glow or spark on top. That's the good shit.

Cake is universal—probably the most universal—like relationships, life, people, community, all layered with how they adapt their own recipes. The best cakes come from the best ingredients and the patience of the bakers and the balance of it all, just like the recipe for a relationship and life shared with someone, or just yourself.

Your CAKE, layered with all the ingredients of you. This is my CAKE I share with you, layered with **C**ommunity **A**nd **K**indness and everything **E**xtra.

The journey in writing this manuscript took form like a cake does. I started with a plate, my iPad, if you will, writing the story in the notepad section—each chapter would be layered. The process, once in the hands of the publishers, the same, layering so that all the ingredients make sense, with the cover being the icing on top.

I love knowing how things get developed from their camera flash. There is always a method to my madness, my logic and how it all connects—it must have meaning.

CAKE, my journey, was created the day I was born, I just had to live it. My published story does not include names. The personal names are not as important as the life I had with each one individually. This is my story. Their names are for their story.

The book cover was chosen with the utmost attention to the parts of me that are my passion, my light, my love.

Gold lettering in the title CAKE was to honour my family, my children, my love for life, it is Golden.

The white cover is to honour all those signatures in chalk, who with love, gave to the cause through The Closet Door.

The back cover in black writing was in honour of The Closet Door's "chalkboard of supporters" home of all the love from supporters who wrote upon it. Leaving a mark in my heart.

I truly hope CAKE will leave a mark and you will always know…

…You Matter.

Chapter 18
Classic CAKE

"Good morning, Vietnam"

This was Robin Williams in one of his classic roles, with his classic voice.

I could identify with this profound comedic genius. Most could. More so, as a child growing up, I could identify with anyone odd, different from the norm, against the grain. It was his character Mork. He was quite the man of talents, as I grew and started to follow him in movies and TV spots. I loved the real Robin and not just the stage presence. I loved the snippets of him and his mom; I found warmth from them as my mom was ill. I took comfort in them, and they helped me through this experience. I wonder how much that brought solace to their own lives, as much as he brought to mine.

I value everything about this man. He made it ok to be crazy with laughter and show your spark. You mustn't lose it. Ever. He made me smile and laugh; the laughing made a positive impact. He created a world where being your true self was valued. There is comfort in laughing; there is comfort in the company you laugh with.

Sometimes, the simple guidance I give myself while looking in the mirror is this: our soulmate knows us best, which is us. I laugh. I laugh thinking about all that I've gone through—schooling, life skills—you don't need any of these to clean toilets, yet here I am. Instead of starting from the ground up, I am starting from the toilet bowl up. Making it a royal flush. It's ok. I'm ok. I just laugh, slowly. The best days happen every day when I wake up, the moment I open my eyes and I'm still here.

Yes, I often question myself, I have self-doubts, and then I look at all the lessons I have learned. Love is the answer, "they" say. Question, who is "they?" And how do they know? "They" say "don't burn the candles at both ends," but I've never seen a candle burning at both ends. Perhaps "they" have?

Questions are part of my life—I'm a need-to-know girl. I go down many rabbit holes or general thoughts. I thought I would share just one of these with you, seeing as you're just so excited to hear one of them and you may have questioned this, too. "Why is the sky blue?" If the sun is so bright, should it not shine yellow? Like I said, just a thought. Curious, as an over-thinker, one thought turns into many.

The laughter is the heart saying it will get better.

… the laughter is the better.

There are forms of laughter, banter being one of them, one of my favourites. It shines from something inside the soul, for me anyway, it makes me feel my words are appreciated, my humour valued and validated as funny. It's a connection and gives a charge. It makes me feel human. Relatable. When I laugh, my whole soul laughs, and then my soul must use the laugh powder room. The best laugh on screen must be from the original Disney *Mary Poppins* movie in the "I love to laugh" scene.

My mom had such an infectious laugh. Sometimes it would come abruptly, and sometimes I could sense its intro. She would have made a perfect live studio audience, a one-woman audience. I think she should have bottled it and shared it with the world.

Standing ovation.

Chapter 19
CAKE Toppers

"Please don't worry so much, because in the end, none of us have very long on this earth."

—Robin Williams

In 2014, I was in a car accident. A drunk driver T-boned us on the way home from our vacation in the States. I was rushed to the hospital. Before the ambulance arrived, I was lying there, feeling that I was taking my last breaths. All I could see was the other drivers and thirty-one shopping totes; it looked like direct selling blowout sale.

They took me, in my bathing suit with a neck brace on and strapped to the gurney—picture that, if you will. It may not have been the best attire, or so I thought. The paramedic was about to give me morphine and said, "tell me if the pain worsens." Wait, what? I can't tell you if anything worsens if I'm on morphine. We arrived after what seemed to be hours, and the doctor leaned over me because of the neck brace, which by the way, was a pain in the neck. I couldn't believe my eyes. Then more came to my bedside, and they looked like disciples from heaven, gorgeous men. I asked if I was dead or on the show *Grey's Anatomy*. He laughed, of course, I'm funny. He replied, "Neither," and they would have to cut my bathing suit off for cat scans and X-rays. So, what I'm hearing is that a band of brothers in the hallway of a hospital was going to undress me and robe me. I didn't know at that moment, until hours went by, morphine had everything to do with that moment.

Even up to what I thought was my dying day, there were laughs.

Mammograms: the boobie trap is what I call it. I went in for a scheduled appointment, on a call back for an ultrasound. What ended up happening was blinding. But how? Well, I'm going to tell you. First off, I have a fear of hospitals. But it's because every time I'm there, something else happens. This day didn't prove me wrong.

My sister did tell me to bring someone with me. She was right.

They needed to put dye in me to do an x-ray. During the last moments after, I had to sit. I was looking at a picture and in moments, some of it vanished. What is happening? The technician looked at me, she was faceless. I said, "I'm going blind." I started to panic. How could such a test make me go blind. I couldn't even google anything. I was blind— both eyes clouded over, with just a hint of vision.

They put me in a wheelchair and wheeled me down to the emergency department. Yes, I ended up in emergency, going blind, on an already stressful day. I got them to call the Foundation office, which resided in the hospital. I had a relationship with the staff through many years of gifting donations for cancer care. I was so happy to hear the sweet voice of one of the staff moments later. I just laughed and said, "I'm blinded by the fact that I have no idea what's going on."

She was present for me and went to find out the possibilities of what I was experiencing. Sure enough, I was so stressed and anxious, I sent myself into an acute migraine. An acute migraine lasts about twenty minutes and then sight slowly becomes clearer, and what follows is a massive headache. That's exactly what happened.

I took my anxiety to a whole new level.

Well, because self-love is important to me, I forgave myself, gave myself a pep talk. I took myself out for a coffee, a Tylenol, and a soak in the tub. Some real "Calgon, take me away" moments.

No matter how you slice your CAKE, do it with humour.

Chapter 20
I Love CAKE!

In life, there are many people who will pick up your book, your life, and run their finger down the pages, exposing your weaknesses. Then there are those who will skim through the chapters, folding the corners on what they find intriguing.

Then there are the ones who come along and read its every word, chapter by chapter. Those who go back, reading the most important moments, seeing your tears, coffee stains, and heartache, but also seeing the passion, the vulnerabilities, and your light.

It is these people who keep the book.

I have been writing and journaling for over two years. Late nights to early mornings, pull-over-to-the-side-of-the-road moments, and parking in mall plazas. My car became my writing nook. Writing thoughts down while bouncing in and out of local coffee shops, drinking copious amounts of coffee. All this writing is now taking shape in its very own book.

The first to read it was my daughter. It was such a nervous feeling. Not only is she a saviour in my world, but she was also now reading from my eyes.

She cried. It also made her laugh, smirk, and look up with proud eyes.

She will keep my book.

My best friend: he not only walks beside me, but also carried me through some rough patches. He created a safe house, he saw me raw, he saw the wild card in me that came with a soft heart, and he saw the light that sparked. He shared my love for The Closet Door, local community passion, as well as the stage, sharing the mic. I know we will always be connected as soul friends. I am forever grateful. He has blessed me with the honour of standing up on stage, but this time for his wedding, with his beautiful angel wife. Together they created a beautiful baby girl, a sweet lamb from God. They gave me the honour of being her fairy god-mother—the announcement came with a wand, scroll, and wings. I vowed unconditional love, my bond as bold as my friendship with her parents.

The Closet Door opened, and when it closed, we followed the chalk line together, beyond the brick and mortar.

He will keep my book.

Another beautiful friend: she walked the path with me, had my back, and gave me her unconditional love. It was a balanced friendship, a nurturing friendship. She loves to share in her stories; they often start with "to make a long story short." Those short stories were the long versions. I loved them all, and her giving heart. She is my vibrancy and light. She is my Mama T. She is very special to a lot of people. She is love. She will always have a chair at my table.

She will keep my book.

The girlfriends: they embrace the crazy side of life, and at times laugh so hard we need to leave the situation to breathe. They came into my world like lightening. They were wild cards who remind me every day that I am important, loved, worth it; some even read pages from my book, and encouraged its journey. Our friendships are important, we support each other, and we've made a pact to each other—we will always be ready to ride at dawn.

They will keep my book.

To my Betty: we sat together on the stoop, our stoop in our neighbourhood; it held a lot of memories. We experienced a lot together. We went through all the moments of marriage, raising our children, embracing our single lives. We went from watching our favourite weekly television shows to lawn talks, to hustling in our careers. Our relationship outlasted the marriages on our street, including our own. I will always be your Veronica.

She will keep my book.

The community saw my passion, and wanted, in some way, to make a positive impact; they simply, at times, needed to feel the vibe that The Closet Door created from all those a part of its warmth and compassion.

The community partnerships that evolved through The Closet Door, the efforts I presented—they saw me, they believed in me, as I believed and saw their value. They were on board in every way. It's unsaid that they would always help me with my voice, my passions. In a heartbeat.

Professionally and personally. Many are starting out on their own entrepreneurial ships, sailing into photography, music, the arts. I support them all; they, too, shared the stage with me. Such beautiful humans.

The volunteers: they gave more than their time; they gave their hearts and compassion. They wanted to enrich their lives, to see the possible, to manifest bigger roles for the future. They were incredibly powerful, each in their own way. In some way, The Closet Door turned on the light and allowed them to create their own sun. Planted and growing in all this goodness, human kindness was the water.

Like on the hit television series *Friends*, it was built like our very own Central Perk. But ours, a true story.

They will keep my book.

My family: the most unconditional love, the fuel that helps me to be better, do better, whatever and however that forms in life. God knows and they know that I will do what I feel in my soul, not because I'm stubborn, but because I'm passionate.

You really can do anything you put your mind to. Failing doesn't mean failure; it means you tried. I don't see anyone holding a measuring tape to measures my life's values or experiences.

Your experiences are real. No one can take your words from you.

My family knows that, embraces that, encourages me.

They will keep my book.

Chapter 21
The CAKE Batter

Hey guys, how was the foot traffic to get here? You all look so ready to have a good time—let's make that happen!!

At night, I like to drift off with people, just as much as waking up to them. So, this is what I do when I am anxious and feel like I need to take myself to a place of comfort.

I imagine myself surrounded by people, and in my imagination,

a studio downtown, like a Speaker's Corner. The crowd surrounds me. The windows are clear, and the speaker is behind the glass, heard by those that surround it. Everyone listens and most interact.

I make conversations with them as I host the show—my co-host, coffee.

Sometimes I end the studio shows with, "May an angel kiss you as you sleep, may their wings tickle your nose." Or "May your day be strong and your coffee stronger."

Shortly after that, I am asleep, sometimes before the goodnight sign off.

We all have these things that calm us. I needed more ease.

I took the time to get to know the stages that I went though as I grew to be the woman I am now. I sectioned it off by stage of development—child, teen, adult, mid-life—to see how my personal traits changed.

What is surprising is all the weaknesses I needed to work on. This helped me to visually measure how I grew, and what changes my life made over time.

I thought the CAKE chart was perfect—I could see the ingredients that made me and needed to be adjusted for full flavour. The "bake-off," seeing all the ingredients through the years, helped me to pull out my weaknesses and evolve them into strengths. It helped me; you're never too old to bake a CAKE.

The ingredients that made me were mixed in this bowl of life.

As a child, I was defiant, stubborn, impulsive, curious, shy, people-pleasing, imaginative, afraid of abandonment.

As I grew to a be teenager, I had low self-esteem and a strong work ethic. I was people-pleasing, independent, empathetic, a team player, easily influenced, with a dash of naivety.

In adulthood, I became a young mother and a college graduate. I was a perfectionist, a people-pleaser, empathetic, over-thinker, team player, independent, sensitive, easily influenced, naive, anxious, depressed. I still lacked self-confidence, and still had abandonment issues, but I valued others, and contained a whole bag of kindness.

In mid-life, I was bold like coffee, and my sense of self-worth was stronger. I was sensitive, confrontational, inspirational, passionate, fierce, focused, successful, confident, curious, entrepreneurial, independent. I was a hometown hero, a community kindness recipient, a survivor, and an author.

This CAKE batter at times was hard to swallow—I could see the pain I carried at most stages.

Gaining perspective means seeing the gains.

The stage I am in now is where I stand loved.

I have never been completely loved by me...

... till now.

I matter.

Chapter 22
Surprise CAKE

This is where I sit down with gratitude. I am blessed with these memories, through real-life camera flashes.

The moment of lining up and being a go-go dancer contender on Kelly and Regis's show in New York.

The same day, I ran into the host of *Tiny Talent Time* on the streets of Manhattan, who was working for a news station, asking people on the street if they liked surprises. I remember telling him I watched his show growing up. I asked if could he snap his finger while asking me the question like he did when he used to ask the children on his show. He would say, "If I could snap my fingers and have your wish come true, what would it be?" Every time I answered, "my own room," which was bizarre because I was afraid of being alone—finally, he put the mic up and I said, "I love surprises like you, you were my surprise today!"

Turns out it wasn't him. I realized it when I looked him up while writing this book, to see when he worked for a TV station in New York. Bill Lawrence only worked for

CBC and Canadian television. Hilarious, mind blown—for almost fifteen years, I have been telling that story. I laughed so hard, and at the same time I was filled with sweet sadness.

I remember, in my thirties, entering Disney World for the first time. The smells of the candy, being in the bubble of endless magic. I remember the time we were VIPs, on the spot to meet American Idol winners. I was chosen with my oldest son to experience this memory, at the opening of "The American Idol Experience." He was quite the fan, and the next day he tried out for show as a contestant; after the second audition, they thanked him for his efforts, and he thanked them for the opportunity.

Years before in LA, ten glorious days with my sister—our trip a gift from my dad. We ended up sharing a hotel with past American Idol season (though in the current TV season) contestants! We met at the most beautiful, intimate, outdoor hotel lounge.

We almost had them give my sister's book to Ellen, as she was a judge at this time. They said they don't really see the judges off-stage. We asked this one contestant to tap her nose and we would know the song was dedicated to us— omg, we had so much fun, even the drinks winked at us!

Other memories include ringing in the new year in New York City at Dick Clark's Rockin' New Year's Eve in Times Square. My husband at the time, and our three children, made our way to be there for noon. We stood by the Olive Garden in Times Square. All roads leading to Times Square were blocked off—each section opened to Times Square.

It was incredible to see the process, the different stages, all in Times Square, for different television stations. Miley

CAKE

Cyrus played that year as the main entertainer. It was brisk. We had a couple of waters, as apparently you cannot leave your spot, even to go to the bathroom. We drank sparingly. Like little birdies all lined up on a twig, passing waters.

We stayed in the same spot for twelve hours. All squeezed in like sardines. I will say we had a blast, and we were in good spirits. The crowds went on for miles; it was social fuel for me. I met everyone around me by the time it was over. We grabbed some numbers, took loads of selfies, and saved the red, white, and blue confetti squares. I framed these when I got home a couple days later. We met a couple and their twenty-one-year-old daughter. They told us that twenty-one years earlier, they were at Times Square, and she was in her mom's tummy. They were from Italy. They didn't realize the cold was so chilly and were not quite prepared. We shared our blankets and "hot pockets." I had packed like I'd be hiking for days on a survival trip, so I was prepared for these moments.

The best moments are better than any ball drop. They are the lives I created, lambs of God. The births of all my children.

Gone are the days where I took the kids shopping at Christmas time, filling the cart with the toys they wanted, and then taking the cart to lay away. I would tell them that's where Santa picks up the toys; that's how he knows what you truly want. They loved that, and then asked more questions—I'd change the subject and get them a treat (my creative juices sometimes run out, so for everything else, there's Smarties).

My heart was so proud of my daughter—she was a recipient chosen for a "Kids Can Care" event, for donating to cancer care. She was nine. I remember making file folders filled with all their achievements; the moments on stage and performing on the ice and baseball fields. Celebrations of new beginnings and growth.

I remember moments when they crawled into my bed, tiny and scared like I used to be. We upgraded from a queen bed to a king, and gum wasn't allowed.

I remember the vows and the pain of leaving my first marriage. My survival came from a natural fight in me. At times, taking even the smallest items to cash converters, for money. I remember crying endless nights wondering when I would see better days—overthinking, anxious, many nights crying, ashamed, like I failed everyone, to the point of anxiety attacks, being rushed to the hospital, thinking I was dying.

After my second marriage, I poured my energy into charity events and church. I got to the point where I was living off a credit card for survival—I got the credit card by signing up to get a free blue jays T-shirt at one of their games.

I struggled a lot. I started taking accountability and responsibly for my faults. No one is perfect, and with the challenges in this world, I'm sure each of us displays mental exhaustion sometimes.

A mental breakdown brought me a mental breakthrough.

Starting from the ground up, I learned a lot; I learned that material items are not attached to survival, the bare necessities are. I did find a job locally, someone who had entrepreneurial passions like myself. I was Director of

Communication, doing marketing and helping nurture his business. I couldn't afford much; I became adaptable to the thrift life. Sometimes I grabbed extra napkins from fast food places and used them as coffee filters and paper towel when I couldn't afford to buy them. I used bread twist ties (the one with the dates on them) to fix my flip flops. I used clothing as towels when I was first on my own after my first separation; my dishes were paper plates and solo cups, and plastic red Coca Cola glasses. At least they went with the theme of my dollar store kitchen table cover on my plastic curb-side patio table.

All those things had a purpose; they were still useful. Most important, I had myself and my kids, and the surroundings or material items or the environment don't matter. They don't define you.

I got on the track to continue the marathon once again, and once I did…

… I applied for a consumer proposal for the credit card, and let me tell you, that ended up being an expensive Blue Jays T-shirt, but it covered me during my survival.

Chapter 23
Sweetie Bakery

I don't ever have to defend my truths; I never have to justify my actions. It only needs to make sense to me. I put in a lot of work.

I never even asked for validation. I never asked anyone what they thought of me, and no one really told me. I never fully shared my story; I didn't lean or show my raw emotions or fears to anyone. No one saw all the Band-Aids.

One day, my sister saw me through the healing process. I was now on my own after the marriages and the relationships, on my healing path, refueling. Life is not fair—it was never promised to be. I was now given the opportunity to make me better, without the Band-Aids.

She started off with, "Sweetie." (She called me that from the time we went to LA—I love it.) I took a sip of my coffee and listened.

She told me how proud she was of me, how strong a woman I was, and my strong courage was.

She will never know how many Band-Aids came off that day. How much fuel she gave me.

She will keep the book.

… because I will gift her one and because she will read it, love it. She loves her Sweetie.

I often think, if I hadn't gone through what I went through, where would I be?

Or, am I supposed to be—this very second—on my birthday, finishing up this CAKE?

Yes, you can have your cake and eat it, too.

The moment we pour into ourselves is like the icing on a cake. We will see the rejuvenation of our souls. I'm going to say yes—my faith, my hope, my lessons, my turbulence, my triumphs, my gratitude, my chaotic comforts, my strength, my losses, my empath heart, my entrepreneurial mind, and vision have made it so that I am on the path I have chosen. I hope one day you'll feel the magnet pull to your purpose.

I have the chance to branch these qualities to help human beings, making more of an impact. Some attributes I was born with, and some needed to blossom. I asked God for guidance on many occasions, and then I started to look for the opportunities. God can't come to earth just to give you what you ask for—you must put in the work.

It's your journey, not his.

Take the footsteps.

Light the Jesus candle!

Chapter 24
Make a Wish and Blow Out the Candles

In each moment that passes, my future is in front of me. I know that when we meet, the pieces of my present will fit into yours. You will test me even more; at times my sensitive heart will be stronger, my anxiety more patient, waiting for my future moments. I will embrace my whole self. I will live in the moment, with coffee of course!

I have embraced my purpose, through **C**ommunity **A**nd **K**indness and everything **E**xtra.

It's about going forward, to be better and do better, from the inside out.

I don't have regrets. I don't have baggage (I'm not packing my bags with the past). I have life experiences and challenges that I have accepted or blessed and released. I'm built to live the most authentic life; my purpose and passion speaks that.

If it feels good and makes you happy, it doesn't have to make sense to others.

Who's one person who has been with you from day one, who's always stood by you, has gotten you into trouble, and out of trouble. Made good choices and bad ones. Been there when you have fallen, weak, and has built you up with inner strength, who gives you fuel when you say, "I can't go on," or "I'm not worth it," who fills your cup, pushes the button, and makes you coffee in the morning. Who says, "you can do it," and reaches to lift you up.

It's you. Treasure you. Take care of you.

It took me 17,520 days of my life to get to truly see my value.

Sometimes I go back to a memory of my moments, being so fueled by being me. Returning to a childhood memory, and how I used to jump on my bed and all around my room floor stepping on records not in their sleeves, and just yelling how much I loved the whole world, my family, my friends, my hair, my hands, my face, even right down to my belly button. None of this costing one cent. That little musical snack; I think of it often. She's still inside, loving it all the same.

Humour helps the nerves, and as I am about to have these slices of me read by the world, my world, the public, my city, I thought about how people can use this book.

This book has so many multi-functional features, I thought I'd list some.

1. Use it as a coffee coaster.

2. Use it to prop up your phone for TikTok videos, using the fan-out feature.
3. Use it to help bring calm or to have enhanced cravings for coffee and CAKE.
4. Call a director to get it made into a Netflix series.
5. A man from a small town, with a dog, will read it and search to find me, using posters on poles, looking for the modern-day Cinderella with her one Converse shoe. Yes, I'm on Facebook, so it may be easier—but it's my hallmark moment, and it's my story.
6. All the above.

But it could also be read for the sole purpose of treasuring your own recipe, with all its ingredients in your CAKE—then make a wish and blow out the candles.

"Yes, she's the one." She smiles and looks at her reflection in the mirror, and through her green eyes, to her soul, she says with a wink, "I love your pink lipstick."

I will keep my book.

Licking the Fork

What makes us whole is ourselves. We decide the ingredients that go into us.

There will always be ups and downs, chaos and confusion. Some ingredients that will not be needed; it's a learning process. What leaves a good taste, and what leaves a bad one.

Our lives are always going to be changing. Try and find comfort in your CAKE.

Go with your passions in what serves you, and by doing that, you will help serve you and others, in balance. Don't pull the door when it says push!

I'm telling you, the next partner I have in my life, their energy will match mine. A partnership, like a light bulb and a light switch, working together.

Both of us holding value.

This may be a lot of coffee beans talking, and I may be starting from
the ground to the grind up, but I will tell you, I'm still smiling. I still hold my value—no one can take it. Value is your lifetime ownership.

"God will not have his work made manifest by cowards."
—Ralph Waldo Emerson.

In other words, life is short, cut the crap, manifest, chase your dreams, do the work, have faith, and keep going.

I will give nothing less than everything.

If I allowed people to control my passions, my purpose, and my positive impacts, human lives would not have been impacted on any level, including my own.

I will continue to share the slices of my life…

"…with a pink kiss and a promise."

Piece of CAKE.

The End

…will always reach for a new beginning.
A Monologue by
T.J. Hunt
January 31, 2022

About the Author

T.J. is a mom, daughter, sister, friend, educator, social influencer, philanthropist, community entrepreneur, and hometown hero.

CAKE is T.J.'s debut novel sharing the pieces of her journey through childhood, relationships, motherhood, marriages, online dating, loss, triumph over tragedy, community kindness, and love.

Her fourties' gave light to taking ownership of her passions, value, and self worth. She wants to share this journey of light, to inspire your life through CAKE.

"The only thing I take when I leave this earth is my heart, and I want it full!"

T.J. Hunt

CPSIA information can be obtained
at www.ICGtesting.com
Printed in the USA
BVHW050926110922
646514BV00004B/14